(Below) Rocket-firing 'Typhoons' attacking enemy tanks

CONTENTS

THE STORY OF
Arms and Armour

by EDMUND HUNTER

with illustrations
by ROBERT AYTON

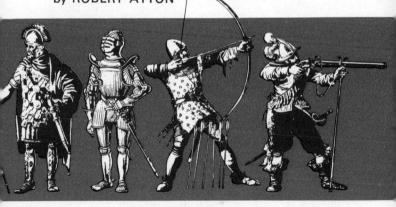

Publishers: Ladybird Books Ltd . Loughborough
© Ladybird Books Ltd (formerly Wills & Hepworth Ltd) 1971
Printed in England

In the beginning

From earliest times man has needed to defend himself, his family and his home, first from the attacks of wild animals—and later from aggressive human beings. Many of the animals were larger and stronger than himself, and it was not until man learned how to use some sort of weapon that he could really be sure of a chance of survival.

Early man's first weapons were those that most easily came to hand. He picked up stones from the ground and fashioned rough clubs from the branches of trees. As his intelligence developed, he found that larger stones could be thrown with great force if he used a sling made of animal skin.

He discovered that his club became more deadly if he tied a sharpened stone to one end to form an axe-like implement. He also learned how to make a thrusting spear with a sharpened or flint-tipped end.

These primitive weapons were in use many thousands of years ago, but even in that distant age they were divided into two basic types: the missile (stone or spear) which could be aimed at an animal or enemy some distance away, and the strike—or shock—weapon (club) for use at close quarters.

0 7214 0296 8

From stone to metal

As the centuries passed, our early ancestors began to develop other weapons of the shock and missile types. They used a bow that could shoot flint-headed arrows. By the late Stone Age (about 7000 BC) they had gained considerable skill in shaping and polishing flint heads for axes, spears and arrows, and in fitting them to the shafts.

Early man lived in small family groups, wandering from place to place in search of food and shelter. Later, several groups joined together to form a tribe, and in time these tribes grew larger and formed into communities, each with its own area of land to develop and protect. The first civilisations appeared in the Middle East, particularly in Egypt and Mesopotamia around 5000 BC, and later in Susa and Sumer. The people learned how to grow crops and raise cattle, and many of them built and lived in towns.

It was necessary for them to protect their towns from aggressors and invaders, and when metals were discovered it became possible to produce much more efficient weapons. Copper was the first metal to be used, but this proved to be too soft. Later, bronze was produced by mixing copper with tin, and a new weapon —the metal sword—came into being.

During the following centuries the knowledge of how to produce bronze and bronze weapons spread northwards from the Mediterranean area as tribes migrated across Europe. By about 2000 BC tribes armed with bronze weapons were invading and settling in Britain.

Mould for
casting Axehead

The first soldiers

With the further development of national life, trained fighting men were needed to give protection against larger and larger numbers of invaders. Soldiers were trained to fight shoulder to shoulder in a *phalanx* so that a shower of arrows or spears could hit the enemy, or a massed attack with swords. Increased weapon-power made necessary some form of protection for the soldiers, so they began to wear special headgear and clothing, and carried a shield to ward off arrows and take the blows from close-quarter weapons.

The Assyrians (who we read about in the Bible) wore leather which was covered in strips of metal to give extra protection. They had helmets, made sometimes of copper but mostly of the tougher bronze.

About this time, a battle was sometimes decided by individual combat between a champion of either side. The famous Biblical story of David and Goliath is a good example of this. It will be remembered that following the defeat of Goliath by David's slingstone, the whole Assyrian army fled from the Israelites.

Greek soldiers at the time of the battle of Marathon (491 BC) were very well equipped. The infantrymen, known as *hoplites*, were armed with a thrusting spear and short sword. Each wore a complicated metal helmet which protected the head, back of the neck and much of the face, and which was frequently topped by a decorated crest. Body armour consisted of a hinged breast and backplate, shaped to follow the wearer's muscles, and a thigh-length leather skirt to which metal strips were attached. Metal leg-protectors were often worn. A round shield, made of leather, wood and metal was carried.

8

Above: David and Goliath
Below: Greek arms and weapons

The discovery of iron

Iron began to replace bronze about 1500 BC, another development which commenced in the Middle East.

At first this new metal was too expensive for general use. The Hittites—a powerful group of people living in Asia Minor and Syria—had discovered how to produce iron from iron-ore. They kept their knowledge a closely-guarded secret, and their iron was so prized by other countries that the Egyptians sometimes paid them in gold four times the weight of iron.

However, in 1283 BC the Hittites were defeated and their country over-run. Many iron-workers fled to other countries, and over the years their knowledge of iron-working spread northwards and eastwards from the Mediterranean. As more and more people became expert at producing and working iron, weapons became more efficient, more numerous and more varied.

By 200 BC tribes invading Britain from the Continent were well-equipped with iron swords and daggers, and iron-tipped spears and arrows. These weapons were far superior to the bronze ones of the tribes who had previously invaded and occupied Britain.

A British Iron Age hill fort under attack

Roman arms and armour

Over a period of about eight hundred years, between 400 BC and 400 AD, the great Roman legions conquered most of the then known world. Their soldiers were armed, as were the Greeks, with a spear, or *pilum*, and a sword. The pilum was a fairly heavy weapon and was usually used for throwing as a missile rather than for thrusting, its steel head being capable of piercing through two shields and any body armour. A volley of pila could break the front line of an opposing phalanx and the attack was then followed-up with swords.

Roman armour changed in detail from time to time, but always consisted of a metal helmet, a tunic of metal-covered leather, and a wood and metal shield. The armour itself was of three basic types: *scale*, *mail* and *lorica*. Scale armour was made by fixing together a series of over-lapping metal plates to a leather tunic. Mail, or chain-mail, was quite a complicated arrangement of metal rings. Each individual ring was interlaced with others and the ends joined by rivetting, the whole assembly being then made into a tunic and worn over a leather under-tunic. Lorica armour consisted of metal strips which fitted around the legionary's chest and waist and joined to other strips which were shaped to fit over the shoulders. Leather was again worn beneath.

Left: A Roman centurion
Right: A Roman legionary

Mounted soldiers

Speed is often important in the winning of a battle and this fact was realised as long as five thousand years ago. The first mobile soldiers were mounted on chariots drawn by horses. However, so far as is known, the horse itself was not used as a mount until nearly two thousand years later.

Chariots were used by the ancient Egyptians, the Assyrians, the Romans and many other peoples. They were light, two-wheeled vehicles having the minimum of bodywork and usually being drawn by two horses. They often carried a driver and one or two soldiers who would attack the enemy at high speed, using bows and arrows and spears. Sometimes chariots had a knife attached to the axle of each wheel, to cut the legs off anyone who dared to approach too closely.

Alexander the Great made very effective use of horsemen in his famous battles. His cavalry units would be stationed on the flanks of the infantry phalanxes, ready to charge into action with lance and sword when the enemy line was pierced. Later, the Gothic barbarians employed different tactics, using heavily-armed cavalry as assault troops. In 378 AD they defeated the Roman army at Adrianople by these means, and in doing so changed the art of war.

Above: Sumerian chariot (3000 BC)
Centre: Egyptian chariot (1330 BC)
14   Below: Greek chariot (550 BC)

The Vikings

Famous for their longships and daring raids across the North Sea, the Vikings began attacking Britain in 793 AD. They were great warriors and were armed with a variety of weapons. The spear and club were commonly used but these invaders also carried a broad-bladed sword about three feet in length. Many of these swords were very well made and greatly prized by their owners, who sometimes named them after their most exciting exploits. Vikings also used two different kinds of axe: a short-handled axe for throwing, tomahawk fashion, and a long-handled axe with a big, curved blade which was wielded in the hands. Another weapon was a type of knife made in various sizes and known as a *scramasax*.

The Vikings were not only well armed but also well armoured. They wore metal helmets which were sometimes fitted at the sides with horns or decorative wings. Their bodies were often protected by tunics, or *byrnies*, of chain-mail. Shields served a double purpose; they were used in the normal way in battle but during a sea voyage they would be hung along the sides of the longships to protect the men while they were rowing. These shields were usually made of wood and strengthened with iron bands, a dome-shaped portion in the middle allowing room for the warrior's hand.

16

The Battle of Hastings

As every schoolboy and ex-schoolboy knows, the Battle of Hastings was fought in 1066. To a great extent it was a battle between the attacking Norman cavalry and the defending English infantry, or *huscarles*, who formed up behind a wall of shields and hacked at the invaders with long-handled axes. The English fought very bravely and possibly lost the battle when, having broken up an enemy attack, the huscarles chased the retiring Normans too far, leaving their own flanks exposed. The cavalry charged again and again at the weakened English and finally won the day. Norman infantry, supporting the cavalry attacks, fired their arrows at random into the air. As they fell, these upset the concentration of the English troops.

Norman cavalry were armed chiefly with heavy lances and long, cutting swords. Armour consisted of a pointed metal helmet with protective nose-piece, or *nasal*, a mail hood, or *coif*, and a knee-length mail byrnie. The byrnie was slit front and back, enabling the wearer to ride his horse.

The huscarles, who always rode into battle but fought on foot, wore armour similar to the Normans. They used kite-shaped shields which could be stuck into the ground leaving both hands free to wield their heavy axes. They also used a heavy throwing hammer, from which the modern athletic field event takes its name.

Norman soldiers (above) and Saxon soldiers (below) of the Battle of Hastings

Armour of the Crusades

The Crusades were a series of nine military operations undertaken by the Christian nations of Europe supposedly to ensure the safe passage of pilgrims travelling through the Holy Land. They covered the period between 1095 and 1211, and many of them were far from successful. The crusading knights were heavily-armoured and needed powerful horses to carry them. They were often clumsy in action and were easily outwitted by the unarmoured *infidels* (non-Christians) on their small, fast ponies.

Crusaders' armour consisted of a helmet which was modified through the years until it completely covered the face and neck. It had a slit to see through and small holes to enable the wearer to breathe. A suit of chainmail covered the whole body. This became very hot under the boiling sun of the Middle East, so the knights wore a cloth *surcoat* over the top of it to prevent the metal becoming too unbearable.

Being completely encased in metal, the knights could not always be recognised, so some wore a crest on the top of the helmet by which they could be distinguished. Later, they added a symbol to their surcoat and shield. In the course of time, these symbols became very colourful and complicated and eventually developed into coats-of-arms. Their use was governed by a strict set of rules, many of which remain in force today.

Above: Crusaders in armour
Below: Saracens on their fast ponies

Plate armour

Against such improved weapons as sharp, well-tempered steel swords, heavy cavalry lances and more powerful bows, chain-mail became less and less effective. To give extra protection, small steel plates were worn at the knees and elbows, and later added to the whole length of the arms and legs. The next development was the breastplate. At first all these separate pieces were worn under the chain-mail, and it was not until the early fifteenth century that *full* suits of plate armour were being used. Even then they were very expensive and only available to the knights and nobles who could afford them. By this time helmets were already being fitted with *visors* which could be swivelled up off the face when not required.

A complete suit of plate armour weighed about half-a-hundredweight but this heavy load was evenly spread over the whole body. Joints between the various pieces were so well made that the wearer could move with surprising freedom. A knight could get up off the ground and mount his charger without assistance: stories about the need for block and tackle to get him on his horse are not always true.

Armoured horses were in use from the twelfth century, metal plates being fitted to their most vulnerable areas to provide protection without preventing the animals from moving freely.

Examples of plate armour

1300   1370   1410   1415

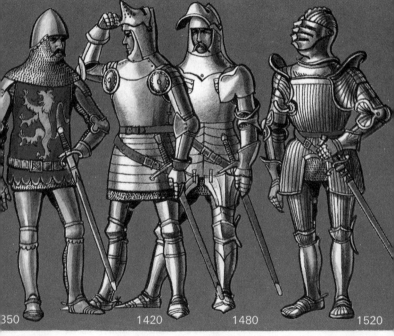

350   1420   1480   1520

1450   1475   1500   1515

The Crossbow

The *crossbow* was in regular use throughout Europe and in the English armies by the beginning of the thirteenth century. Its big advantage lay in the fact that it could be easily handled by untrained soldiers. Early weapons were loaded, or *spanned*, by the archer pulling back the string with both hands while holding down the end of the bow with his foot placed in a type of stirrup. When spanned, the bow was held horizontally in front of the archer who placed a short arrow, or *quarrel*, on the central stock with its end against the string. The bow was then aimed, and fired by means of a trigger.

Later and more powerful models used steel for the actual bow portion instead of wood or horn, and these required other means of spanning. A hook attached to the archer's belt was one method. The string was inserted in the hook and the necessary tension was applied by the archer straightening his back. The most powerful bows of all had to be spanned by mechanical means using a *cranequin* or a windlass to apply the required tension.

Crossbowmen usually carried spare quarrels in a quiver, and had a sword to protect themselves at close-quarters.

The disadvantage of the crossbow is obvious from the above description—it took a long time to prepare for firing.

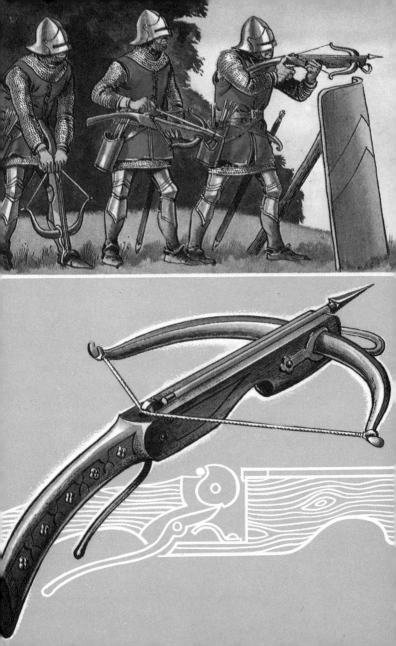

The Longbow

Edward I of England realized the great possibilities of the *longbow* when it was used against him during his wars with the Welsh in the late thirteenth century. It was used on the Continent by Edward III and his son, the Black Prince, at the battle of Crécy (1346) when about 6000 English and Welsh longbowmen defeated an army of French crossbowmen and armoured cavalry greatly superior in numbers. It is said that the English archers fired twelve arrows to every one that the crossbowmen could manage. Apart from inflicting physical damage on the enemy, the noise of so many arrows falling out of the air at the same time frightened the horses. These threw their riders and caused chaos.

The longbow was about six feet in length, up to two inches thick at the centre, and made of yew. The arrows were about three feet long, feathered with goose feathers and fitted with a heavy steel head. Although highly effective in battle, the longbow required considerable strength and skill to use, and the archers needed a great deal of training before they became expert marksmen.

Longbows were mainly defensive weapons, and their success at Crécy and elsewhere was due to the fact that the English were able to choose their own battleground and make the enemy attack toward them.

Longbowmen in action behind sharpened, defensive stakes

Polearms

Polearms, as the name suggests, were arms mounted on poles. They often took the form of a spike combined with an axe-like cutting edge and possibly a series of other spikes. Pikes, poleaxes, bills, partizans and halberds were the most commonly used of this type of weapon. Some of the poles were anything from ten feet to twenty feet in length.

In Europe, the Swiss infantry became expert in the use of polearms during the fourteenth and fifteenth centuries. With massed arrays of pike or halberd points, they broke up enemy cavalry attacks on many occasions. The Swiss were not only successful in defence, however. They were so well trained and so physically fit that, although partly armoured, they could advance quickly on foot for a mile, their pikes held in both hands above their heads with points in the attacking position.

Some two hundred years later, during the English Civil Wars, pikemen were often stationed beside the musketeers to protect them from attack while they reloaded their muskets, a task which took some time and left a musketeer defenceless during the process.

Today, polearms of the partizan type can still be seen in the hands of the 'Beefeaters' on ceremonial occasions in London.

Above: Various polearms
Below: A massed array of polearms opposing a cavalry charge

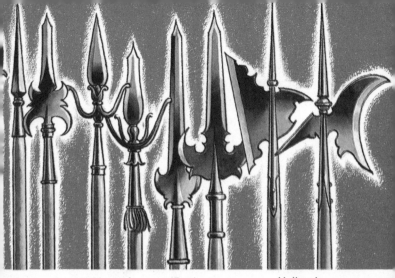

Pikes   Linstocks   Partizans   Halberds

Firearms

The invention of gunpowder, in the early part of the fourteenth century, opened a new chapter in the story of arms and armour. However, progress was extremely slow for many years and often the first cannons were more dangerous to the firers than to those being fired at. They were heavy, cumbersome pieces more suited to sieges than to use on the field of battle. As time went by, shoulder firearms were developed which could be used by individual soldiers, both mounted and unmounted. Late in the fifteenth century they began to replace the cross-bow in Europe and during the next hundred years the English longbow also began to disappear.

Spain was the first country to introduce a one-man firearm that was really effective against armour up to a range of one hundred yards. It was called a musket. It was from three to six feet long, weighed around twenty pounds and was fired from a rest. The first practical pieces of field artillery were introduced into the Swedish army under their warrior king, Gustavus Adolphus (1600–1632). These guns were successful because they were fairly mobile and gun crews were able to keep up with other troops.

The expensively-equipped, highly-trained and heavily-armoured knights of the day thought the new weapons were unfair because they could be handled by common, unskilled soldiers.

Early seventeenth century musketeers and pistol

The end of armour

With the development of shoulder firearms into really useful weapons, and then the introduction of pistols, armour had to be made thicker to give the necessary protection. This was simple enough to do, but as the metal became thicker so it also became heavier. It was more uncomfortable to wear, restricted the wearer's movements and made him very tired. So, in time, he found it necessary to discard the less vital plates. The leg pieces below the knees were the first to go and these were replaced by thick leather boots. Next, half-suits of armour were produced which had no leg plates at all, and the leather boots were sometimes made longer to protect the thighs.

Helmets also became lighter and less enclosing. In England, foot soldiers ceased to use armour after the Civil Wars in the mid-seventeenth century, although breastplates and helmets were still worn by some cavalry units.

With the disappearance of armour, further changes in weapons took place. In cavalry regiments, light lances replaced the old, heavy ones. Regiments also adopted bright and distinctive uniforms. Napoleon used lancers at Waterloo, and British lancers made the famous 'Charge of the Light Brigade' in the Crimea.

A Royalist musketeer surrenders his weapons to Cromwell's Roundheads

A 17th century Wheel-lock Musket

A 17th century Flint-lock Pistol

Swords

Although a great variety of arms were introduced, used and discarded through the centuries, a warrior nearly always carried a sword at his side. It was his personal weapon and, more often than not, his own private property.

Sword design changed considerably as new fashions in armour were introduced and as different battle tactics were adopted. At first, the sword was just a utility weapon, heavy and plain and without a very sharp point or edge. As armour improved, the blade had to be made harder and the edges sharper to penetrate the metal. Points became finer to pierce the narrow gaps between armoured plates. There were single-handed swords, hand-and-a-half swords which could be wielded with one or both hands, and great double-handed swords sometimes five or six feet in length. Some blades were made for slashing, like the Scottish broadsword, or Claymore; others like the long, slim rapiers were intended for thrusting. Other types still were made for cutting or thrusting. The cavalry often used a curved sword known as a sabre.

During the sixteenth and seventeenth centuries the swordsmith's craft reached its peak. The blades of this period were beautifully made of finely-tempered steel. The hilts and the baskets which guarded the hand were often intricately shaped and highly decorated.

Sabre *(cutting)*

Sword *(thrust and cut)*

Cutlass *(thrust and cut)*

Rapier *(thrust and stab)*

Muskets and Bayonets

The design and fire power of muskets gradually improved, although they remained slow to load. Musketeers had to be protected by pikemen for a great number of years. However, to overcome the slow-loading problem on the battlefield, a new tactic was developed in which the musketeers were drawn up several ranks deep. The front rank would fire a volley then retire to the rear of the formation to re-load while the next rank fired, and so on. The muskets themselves changed from wheel-lock and match-lock firing systems to the flint-lock method. The flint-lock ignited the gunpowder by means of a spark and saved the musketeer having to carry a smouldering taper around with him.

An important advance in infantry weapons came with the introduction of the *bayonet* (named after the Bayonne district of France). This was really a short sword with a round handle which could be plugged into the muzzle of the musket. Unfortunately the musket could not be fired with the bayonet in position. Later, a socket fixing arrangement was invented which allowed the bayonet to be fitted to the outside of the barrel, leaving the muzzle clear for firing and loading.

By the year 1700, the infantryman had, in effect, a combined musket and short pike, and the long, heavy pikes began to fade from the battle scene.

Flint-lock Musket

Plug Bayonet 1700

Socket Bayonet 1800

Rifles

Muskets were muzzle-loading weapons. The powder was poured, or dropped in paper cartridges down the bore and packed in tightly with a ramrod. The bullet was dropped in last. The bore was fairly large and quite smooth.

All early rifles were flint-lock muzzle-loaders which fired a spherical bullet. The first cylindrical bullets were used around the middle of the nineteenth century.

Rifles were first used to advantage in battle by the Duke of Wellington's armies on the Continent. Their new weapon had a *rifled* bore: that is to say, instead of being smooth, the bore had a series of grooves cut into it in a gradual spiral extending the whole length of the barrel. The idea of rifling, which of course is still used today, is to give the missile being fired a spinning motion as it leaves the muzzle. It, so to speak, screws itself through the air, and this action helps to maintain a correct course.

The American Civil War of the 1860's saw the development of breech-loading mechanisms which paved the way for further improvements. During the closing years of the nineteenth century, more efficient chemical propulsion materials were discovered to replace gunpowder. This made possible the bolt-action, magazine-loading rifle used by modern infantry.

Federal troops using early rifles in the American Civil War

Ferguson Breach-loading Rifle
(Ball) 1776

Winchester Repeating Rifle
(Cartridge) 1866

Development of artillery

Just as one-man firearms improved so did field guns, but again progress was slow and full of problems. Frederick the Great of Prussia and Napoleon of France made the greatest contributions to the development of artillery tactics. Napoleon in particular realised the value of these weapons and used large, heavy, long-range guns as well as lighter ones which could keep up with the infantry.

Guns at this time were mostly muzzle-loading, smooth-bore types which fired a ball and which ran backward on their wheels each time they were fired. They were not very accurate and had to be rolled forward into position again and re-aimed after every shot. Rifling of the barrel and an elongated shell, were introduced soon after Waterloo. Two other important changes followed later: one was the development of a high-explosive shell which burst on impact, scattering deadly pieces of casing in all directions and capable of inflicting considerable damage. The second major change was the invention of a recoil mechanism which allowed the barrel to move backward after firing while the gun as a whole remained stationary. Breech-loading and automatic cartridge ejection during recoil were added and greatly speeded up the firing rate of these weapons.

By the beginning of the twentieth century, field guns were highly efficient and accurate. They were fitted with a bullet-proof shield to protect the crew.

Early cannons of about 1300–1500

Machine guns and automatic rifles

The idea of firing a large number of missiles in quick succession had exercised the minds of men for many years, and there were certain types of rapid-fire weapons even in the flint-lock era. However, the mechanical problems of such a gun were not properly solved until after the American Civil War. In fact, it was an American who invented one of the first machine guns—the Gatling gun—in 1862. This was not an automatic weapon because it was operated mechanically by means of a handle which had to be turned by one of the crew. The Gatling gun is known to have been used by American troops against the Red Indians. The French also had a mechanically-operated gun called the mitrailleuse.

Another American, Hiram Maxim, who lived in Europe, later designed and produced a completely automatic weapon in which the firing mechanism was actuated by the ammunition itself. Versions of this gun, known in Britain as the Vickers machine gun, were used by both sides with deadly effect during World War I.

Like the Gatling gun, the Maxim was heavy and required some form of transportation as well as a crew to operate it. Light machine guns (LMG's) were developed between the wars. They could be fired from a bipod on the ground or from the hip. Today's infantry-man also uses an automatic rifle to which a bayonet can be attached.

Above: An early British machine gun
Below: An American Gatling gun being used by
British troops in 1880

The Puckle Gun : 1718
The Army authorities were not impressed so the project was abandoned. It was the first British Machine Gun.

The return of armour

After an absence from the battlefield of nearly three hundred years, armour reappeared in 1915 during the First World War when troops on both sides were issued with steel helmets. These helmets varied greatly in style between one country and another, and while none of them were proof against a direct hit from a bullet, they did give some protection against glancing bullets, shell splinters, falling debris, etc.

However, the word 'armour' was soon to take on an entirely different meaning. When the first armoured tank —a British invention—rumbled across the battle-scarred fields of France during the latter part of 1916, a new era of warfare began. Early tanks were slow and not very reliable and it was some time before their true value was realised. It was really between the wars, and more especially during the Second World War, that the full possibilities of armoured vehicles were fully understood. Armoured cars were used for reconnaissance; light and medium tanks were used, like cavalry, for attacking enemy defences and striking deep into occupied territory; heavy tanks often served as highly mobile artillery. Armoured personnel and weapons carriers transported the troops and their equipment into battle.

And so the modern soldier goes to war, not encased in a suit of shining armour, but carried in armoured vehicles which can travel over any ground or even 'swim' in water.

1918 : *A British Mk. IV Tank rumbles ponderously into action at 4 m.p.h.*

1968 : *A British 'Chieftain' riding fast and smoothly across uneven ground at about 40 m.p.h.*

Arms and armour at sea

It seems a strange fact that armour was not used at sea until the end of the Crimean War. The first armoured warship was a French frigate built in 1858. It was made of wood but covered with iron plates four-and-a-half inches thick. Three years later, the first all-iron warship, H.M.S. Warrior, was built for the British Navy. At that time naval guns were fired from fixed positions in the ships' sides, and could not be swivelled one way or the other. Rotating turrets, which allowed the guns to be moved sideways (*traversed*) and up and down, and gave protection to the crew, came into use during the American Civil War. Breech-loading for naval guns replaced muzzle-loading in 1875.

Ships' guns grew rapidly in size and range. Twelve-inch calibre guns, weighing up to forty tons, were common even in the early days. Later, with the advent of light, fast torpedo boats, warships were also provided with smaller, quick-firing guns.

Torpedoes were first used effectively in 1880. Naval submarines capable of firing these missiles were introduced in 1901, although under-sea vessels were invented much earlier.

Today, the most deadly naval weapon is, of course, the Polaris atomic missile. This can be fired from a submerged submarine and can travel enormous distances.

Skirmish between
Frenchman and
Englishman
early 1700's

Nuclear Submarine :
'George Washington'
Armed with 16 Polaris, (A·3s)
with a range of 3000 miles each

In the air

Military aeroplanes were originally employed as spotters for the artillery in the early days of World War I. The pilots were able to see where the artillery shells landed and guide the guns' crews onto their targets. Opposing aircraft would try to chase the spotters away and fighter planes were introduced to protect them. In due course, one force of fighters would meet another and so aerial combat developed.

Some single-seater fighters, with engine and propeller at the front, had a machine gun mounted in the front of the pilot's cockpit. The firing mechanism of the gun was synchronised with the propellor's speed of rotation so that the bullets passed between the blades and did not damage them. In World War II, machine guns and 20mm cannon were mounted within the fighter's wings and some aircraft carried rockets slung below the wings. The pilots were protected by armour-plating fitted around the seat, and by a bullet-proof windscreen.

The first aerial bombs were spherical in shape and they were dropped from airships. Their present cylindrical shape and fins were developed so that they could be carried by aeroplanes and aimed more accurately.

Ground defences were set up to counter attacks from the air, and so anti-aircraft guns were introduced. Today, rockets and guided missiles are among the most important ground-to-air weapons.

48

Above: Aerial combat in World War I
Below: A fighter plane of World War II

The nuclear age

In bygone years man fought animal, then man fought man, and finally army fought army. Few non-combatants were hurt outside the immediate area of the fighting. But times have changed. In World War I, civilians far from the scene of battle became involved and in World War II, many thousands of innocent people were killed and injured by bombs, flying bombs and rockets. Methods and means of warfare are now such that if World War III were to break out no-one would escape the terrible consequences of men's stupid inability to live peacefully together. In all-out nuclear war there can be no winners, only losers. Even children unborn at the time would ultimately suffer from the dreadful effects of atomic radiation.

The nuclear missiles at present available can be launched from the land, from high-flying bombers, from ships at sea and from nuclear-powered submarines of the Polaris type that can cruise non-stop for thousands of miles and remain submerged for several months at a time. To try to prevent the missiles from reaching their targets scientists have produced the anti-missile missile. Also being developed are anti-anti-missile missiles whose object would be to destroy the anti-missiles before they could intercept the missiles. And so the almost insane use of man's skill and resources goes on.

If nuclear war should ever occur, so much of our civilization could be destroyed that if he survived at all, man would, in effect, have to return to the caves from which he tentatively emerged so many thousands of years ago.

The 'Blowpipe' anti-aircraft guided missile

The 'Vigilant' wire-guided anti-tank missile